Pokémon™

NOW YOU SEE IT!

WATCH POKÉMON EVOLVE... RIGHT BEFORE YOUR EYES!

by Simcha Whitehill

SCHOLASTIC INC.

New York   Toronto   London   Auckland

Sydney   Mexico City   New Delhi   Hong Kong

ISBN 978-0-545-45356-1

© 2012 Pokémon. ©1995-2012 Nintendo/Creatures Inc./GAME FREAK inc. TM and ® and character names are trademarks of Nintendo. All Rights Reserved.
Published by Scholastic Inc.
SCHOLASTIC and associated logos are trademarks and/or registered trademarks of Scholastic Inc.

12 11 10 9 8 7 6 5 4 3 2 1   12 13 14 15 16 17/0

Designed by Henry Ng and Two Red Shoes Design
Printed in Malaysia   106
First printing, September 2012

POKÉMON EVOLUTION IN ACTION!

Want to see your favorite Pokémon's Evolutions? Just place your thumb on the outside of this book and start flipping!

- If you put your thumb on the top, you'll see each Pokémon in its pre-evolved form.

- If you put your thumb in the middle, you'll see each Pokémon's first Evolution.

- If you put your thumb on the bottom, you'll see each Pokémon in its final evolved form.

Are you ready? *Now you see it . . .*
Now you don't!

SNIVY

The Grass Snake Pokémon

Height: 2' 00"
Weight: 17.9 lbs.
Type: Grass

Snivy is one of the first Pokémon new Trainers can receive when they visit Professor Juniper's laboratory. And it is one slippery character! Using the sun's rays as its energy source, it can power up and speed off in a flash. Its mind is as quick as its lightning-fast moves.

Ash had a hard time catching this clever Pokémon. Pikachu, Oshawott, and Tepig all turned to mush when Snivy used Attract on them. But luckily, Ash's pal Pidove stood up to Snivy. After chasing the Grass Snake Pokémon up a mountain, over a muddy river, and through the woods, Ash finally added Snivy to his Pokémon crew.

Snivy

Servine

Serperior

SERVINE

The Grass Snake Pokémon

Height: 2' 07"
Weight: 35.3 lbs.
Type: Grass

Just like Snivy, Servine is a master of sneaking up on its opponents. It appears to slither on the ground quickly and quietly, and often camouflages itself in the grass and bushes. Then, when it's ready to strike, it reaches out and surprises its opponents with its long vines.

Snivy

Servine

Serperior

SERPERIOR

The Regal Pokémon

Height: 10' 10"
Weight: 138.9 lbs.
Type: Grass

Serperior has an air of power it rarely needs to display. Like royalty, it carries itself in a way that gets instant respect. While it can usually stop a foe with a single glare, if Serperior meets a worthy adversary, it will snap into battle mode to show who's the boss.

Snivy

Servine

Serperior

TEPIG

The Fire Pig Pokémon

Height: 1' 08"
Weight: 21.8 lbs.
Type: Fire

Tepig is one of the three Pokémon available to brand-new Trainers at Professor Juniper's lab. This Pokémon really earns its classification as a Fire-type — even its nose can shoot fire! But if Tepig ever catches a cold, it snorts black smoke instead.

When Ash found his Pokémon pal Tepig, it blew black smoke in his face because it was sick, skinny, and scared. As it turned out, Tepig had been abandoned outside the Pokémon Battle Club in Accumula Town. Ash rescued it, and the two became fast friends — and one fiery battle team!

Tepig

Pignite

Emboar

PIGNITE

The Fire Pig Pokémon

Height: 3' 03"
Weight: 122.4 lbs.
Type: Fire-Fighting

Pignite is the evolved form of Tepig. When it fuels up with food, the flame in its stomach burns even stronger. That fire inside turns up the heat on its moves, making the Fire Pig Pokémon an even greater foe. The Trainer Bianca always travels with her powerful pal Pignite, known for its blazing Flame Charge.

Tepig

Pignite

Emboar

EMBOAR

The Mega Fire Pig Pokémon

Height: 5' 03"
Weight: 330.7 lbs.
Type: Fire-Fighting

The final evolved form of Tepig, Emboar never has to shave its beard — because it's made of fire! During battle, it can turn its fists into fireballs by lighting them on its chin. But while fiery Emboar may look big and tough in battle, it has a soft side, and would do anything for its friends.

Tepig

Pignite

Emboar

OSHAWOTT

The Sea Otter Pokémon

Height: 1' 08"
Weight: 13.0 lbs.
Type: Water

Oshawott is one of the three Pokémon new Trainers can choose from Professor Juniper's lab. The shell-like scalchop on its stomach may look like a pretty decoration, but it's actually made of a sharp, clawlike material that can be used as a weapon in battle.

Ash first spotted his Oshawott in Professor Juniper's lab. He thought it was adorable, but sadly, it was not his to choose. However, Oshawott had other ideas in mind! It followed Ash and his new friend Iris into the woods and begged Ash to join his traveling crew. Ash asked Professor Juniper if he could train the Water-type, and they've been together ever since.

Oshawott

Dewott

Samurott

DEWOTT

The Discipline Pokémon

Height: 2' 07"
Weight: 54.0 lbs.
Type: Water

The evolved form of Oshawott, Dewott has not one, but two scalchops! Dedicated and determined, Dewott trains hard to master its scalchops, which often spells double trouble for opponents in battle.

When Ash and Pikachu battled Dewott for the first time at the Pokémon Battle Club in Accumula Town, they were incredibly impressed with Dewott's well-coordinated attacks. Looks like Oshawott needs to keep practicing!

Oshawott

Dewott

Samurott

SAMUROTT

The Formidable Pokémon

Height: 4' 11"
Weight: 208.6 lbs.
Type: Water

The final evolved form of Oshawott, Samurott can stop its opponents with a single look. Its piercing battle cry cuts to the very core of its foes, sending them running. But when those scare tactics don't work, Samurott can always rely on its massive sword, which is made from the same armor as its front legs.

Oshawott

Dewott

Samurott

AXEW

The Tusk Pokémon

Height: 2' 00"
Weight: 39.7 lbs.
Type: Dragon

Axew likes to use its tusks to mark its territory on the bark of trees. Sometimes the wood will accidentally break off one of Axew's tusks, but the tusk will grow back in even stronger and sharper than before.

Ash's travel buddy Iris was born in a village that prizes Dragon-types. A wise elder gave her a few-days-old Axew. Just like Ash's Pikachu, Iris's Axew likes to travel outside its Poké Ball — it prefers to hang out in Iris's ponytail.

Axew

Fraxure

Haxorus

FRAXURE

The Axe Jaw Pokémon

Height: 3' 03"
Weight: 79.4 lbs.
Type: Dragon

The evolved form of Axew, Fraxure has tusks that are a force to be reckoned with. They can make solid rock crumble. Unlike Axew, Fraxure's tusks will not grow back after a bad break. So Fraxure makes sure to take good care of their pointy tips by constantly sharpening them on stones.

Axew

Fraxure

Haxorus

HAXORUS

The Axe Jaw Pokémon

Height: 5' 11"
Weight: 232.6 lbs.
Type: Dragon

Haxorus is the final evolved form of Axew. On the outside, its body is covered in a tough armor. It also has super-sharp, bladelike tusks that can shred steel. This Pokémon is known to be nice, but when it comes to battle, it's equipped to defend its territory to the bitter end.

Axew

Fraxure

Haxorus

PIDOVE

The Tiny Pigeon Pokémon

Height: 1' 00"
Weight: 4.6 lbs.
Type: Normal-Flying

These city-dwelling Pokémon like to flock together in urban areas. They are not afraid of people, even if they don't always understand their commands. Ash's Pidove was usually happy to help with searches from its sky-high view, and many Trainers find that a friend that can fly certainly comes in handy! Pidove was the first wild Pokémon Ash caught in Unova.

Pidove

Tranquill

Unfezant

TRANQUILL

The Wild Pigeon Pokémon

Height: 2' 00"
Weight: 33.1 lbs.
Type: Normal-Flying

This wild Pokémon is believed to have a special habitat deep in the woods, where there is no war. Once attached to a Trainer, Tranquill is hard to separate from him or her. No matter where it is, no matter how far away, it can find its Trainer.

Ash's loyal pal Pidove evolved into Tranquill while helping him round up a horde of Venipede crawling around Castelia City. Ash's rival Trip has a Tranquill on hand, too.

Pidove

Tranquill

Unfezant

UNFEZANT

The Proud Pokémon

Height: 3' 11"
Weight: 63.9 lbs.
Type: Normal-Flying

You can spot a male Unfezant by the red plumes on its head, which they use to scare off their foes. These Pokémon are known for being aloof — they refuse to bond with anyone but their Trainers. The females, on the other hand, are known for their superior flying ability.

Pidove

Tranquill

Unfezant

SEWADDLE

The Sewing Pokémon

Height: 1' 00"
Weight: 5.5 lbs.
Type: Bug-Grass

The Sewing Pokémon is all about clothing! This stylish Pokémon is known for its skills as a tailor. It can stitch up its own outfits using leaves and the sticky thread that shoots out of its mouth.

When Ash first encountered his buddy Sewaddle in Pinwheel Forest, it took him by surprise and turned him into a ball of that very thread. But that just made Ash even more determined to catch it!

Sewaddle

Swadloon

Leavanny

SWADLOON

The Leaf-Wrapped Pokémon

Height: 1' 08"
Weight: 16.1 lbs.
Type: Bug-Grass

The evolved form of Sewaddle, this tree-loving Pokémon turns fallen leaves into a special fertilizer that enriches the forests it lives in. Ash's Sewaddle evolved into Swadloon during a battle with the Castelia City Gym Leader, Burgh, and his Whirlipede. Like its pre-evolved form, Swadloon enjoys wearing leaves. When it is chilly, it bundles up in its leaf coat to keep warm.

Sewaddle

Swadloon

Leavanny

LEAVANNY

The Nurturing Pokémon

Height: 3' 11"
Weight: 45.2 lbs.
Type: Bug-Grass

This caring Pokémon keeps its Eggs warm by wrapping them in overripe leaves. Once they hatch, Leavanny weaves clothing for its pre-evolved form, Sewaddle. Leavanny are also known for crafting Pokémon clothing using the silky thread it spins.

When Ash's friend Sewaddle needed a new leaf hood, Burgh's Leavanny fashioned it a fresh outfit out of leaves.

Sewaddle

Swadloon

Leavanny

VENIPEDE

The Centipede Pokémon

Height: 1' 04"
Weight: 11.7 lbs.
Type: Bug-Poison

Venipede can sense what's going on around them by using the pointy feelers on their heads and tails. When they feel a Flying-type Pokémon swooping in, Venipede protect themselves with a paralyzing bite full of poison. Known as the Centipede Pokémon, Venipede make their nests underground.

Venipede

Whirlipede

Scolipede

WHIRLIPEDE

The Curlipede Pokémon

Height: 3' 11"
Weight: 129.0 lbs.
Type: Bug-Poison

The evolved form of Venipede is covered in rock-hard armor. The Curlipede Pokémon spins like a speedy wheel to run over its opponents. While it's better known for its rolling attacks, Whirlipede used a stunning Solar Beam on Ash's Sewaddle during a battle with Castelia City Gym Leader, Burgh. The move helped Sewaddle evolve into Swadloon.

Venipede

Whirlipede

Scolipede

SCOLIPEDE

The Megapede Pokémon

Height: 8' 02"
Weight: 442.0 lbs.
Type: Bug-Poison

Scolipede's looks are deceiving because the huge Megapede Pokémon can be light on its feet. It can charge at its opponents with great speed, and then ram them with its horns.

But although those stripy tail points are prickly, the sharp claws that line Scolipede's neck are just as dangerous — they are also poisonous. In fact, Scolipede is such a fierce fighter that when Iris's Axew accidentally fell on one in the forest, it took Snivy, Tepig, Pansage, Pikachu, and Excadrill to rescue it.

Venipede

Whirlipede

Scolipede

SANDILE

The Desert Croc Pokémon

Height: 2' 04"
Weight: 33.5 lbs.
Type: Ground-Dark

Sandile love to bury their entire bodies — everything except for their eyes and snout — in the hot dunes of the desert. If you look closely, you may spot the tops of these Pokémon sneaking across the desert.

There's one particular Sandile that was happy to make itself known to Ash. After an earlier battle with Ash's Pokémon, this sunglasses-wearing Sandile created an amazing tunnel trap to get the chance at a rematch with Pikachu.

Sandile

Krokorok

Krookodile

KROKOROK

The Desert Croc Pokémon

Height: 3' 03"
Weight: 73.6 lbs.
Type: Ground-Dark

Like its pre-evolved form, Sandile, Krokorok has a thin shield covering its eyes that protects it from the harsh blasts of sandstorms. But this membrane over Krokorok's eyes also has the ability to sense heat, so it can see things even in pitch-black night.

These days, Ash keeps a Krokorok on hand. It's the evolved form of the Sandile that wanted to battle Pikachu. And it still has its sunglasses!

Sandile

Krokorok

Krookodile

KROOKODILE

The Intimidation Pokémon

Height: 4' 11"
Weight: 212.3 lbs.
Type: Ground-Dark

Krookodile's specialized eyes are like built-in binoculars that can focus on things far in the distance. Once it spots and catches some prey, they can't get away. Krookodile's chompers are so strong they can crush a whole car! No Pokémon can escape its terrifying teeth.

Sandile

Krokorok

Krookodile

LILLIPUP

The Puppy Pokémon

Height: 1' 04"
Weight: 9.0 lbs.
Type: Normal

The fluff on this adorable pup's face acts like a supersensitive radar that picks up even the slightest changes to its surroundings.

While it can be fun to pet this cute furball, beware on the battlefield! Brave Lillipup turns into a ferocious fighter. Ash found out just how tough it can be when he and Tepig lost a battle with Lillipup and Lenora, the Nacrene City Gym Leader.

Lillipup

Herdier

Stoutland

HERDIER

The Loyal Dog Pokémon

Height: 2' 11"
Weight: 32.4 lbs.
Type: Normal

The evolved form of Lillipup always listens to its Trainer's directions. It is so obedient that it's often called upon to help train other Pokémon. The fur on its back isn't fun to pet, since it's actually a protective armor. But that hard shell is not Fire-type-proof. During Ash's rematch with Herdier and Lenora, the Nacrene City Gym Leader, Tepig used a fiery Flame Charge to win the round.

Lillipup

Herdier

Stoutland

STOUTLAND

The Big-Hearted Pokémon

Height: 3' 11"
Weight: 134.5 lbs.
Type: Normal

This shaggy Pokémon sports a warm fur coat. The final Evolution of Lillipup, it also has a soft spot for people, especially those in need. Heroic Stoutland is always ready to rescue someone stuck in a blizzard, stranded on a mountain, or even lost at sea. This Pokémon's loyalty and bravery make it a good friend for any Trainer.

Lillipup

Herdier

Stoutland

GOTHITA

The Fixation Pokémon

Height: 1' 04"
Weight: 12.8 lbs.
Type: Psychic

The white bows on Gothita's head are not just for decoration. They are special feelers that increase the Fixation Pokémon's psychic power. But Gothita also like to assess situations with an intense stare that helps them see things no one else can. Gothita's unusual abilities came in handy when Officer Jenny needed help solving the mysterious disappearance of Audino near Nimbasa Town.

Gothita

Gothorita

Gothitelle

GOTHORITA

The Manipulate Pokémon

Height: 2' 04"
Weight: 39.7 lbs.
Type: Psychic

The evolved form of Gothita, Gothorita gets its power from starlight. While everyone else is deep in sleep, it's wide awake, using its psychic powers to move stones through thin air in order to recreate the pattern of the stars in the night sky. But rocks are not all they like to make move! This slick Psychic-type loves to trick people into a trance using hypnosis.

Gothita

Gothorita

Gothitelle

GOTHITELLE

The Astral Body Pokémon

Height: 4' 11"
Weight: 97.0 lbs.
Type: Psychic

The final evolved form of Gothita, Gothitelle has a deep and powerful connection to the universe. Its incredible psychic power can even distort space and reality. In fact, when Ash, Cilan, and Iris encountered Gothitelle on the Skyarrow Bridge, they got caught in a foggy time warp. They experienced Gothitelle's fondest memories of working on a ferryboat before the bridge was built.

Gothita

Gothorita

Gothitelle